19 Keys to Uncommon Solutions

ALSO BY PASTOR WD FAVOUR
Can God Be Lonely?
Healed!
Rivers In The Desert

19 keys to
UNCOMMON SOLUTIONS

How to Unleash Supernatural Waves of Divine Favours in Your Life!

Pastor WD Favour

19 keys to UNCOMMON SOLUTIONS

Copyright © 2011 by:
Pastor WD Favour

ISBN 978-978-914-684-0

Published in Nigeria by:
WILDFIRE PUBLISHING

All rights reserved.
No portion of this book may be used without the written permission of the publisher, with the exception of brief excerpts in magazines, articles, reviews, etc.

For further information or permission, address:

http://www.wdfavour.com/contact
pastorwdfavour@gmail.com

All scripture quotations are from the New International Version of the Bible, except otherwise stated.

*To all the wonderful people of my
spiritual family,
the Citizens Family*

Contents

1st Key | **Develop an Open and Hearing Ear 10**
2nd Key | **Eliminate Every Hindrance to Hearing God's Voice 18**
3rd Key | **Strengthen Your Faith in God 23**
4th Key | **Utilize the Spiritual Weapons of Praying and Fasting 28**
5th Key | **Put Your Foot Down! 32**
6th Key | **Expect Waves Of Favours! 37**
7th Key | **Operate God's Faith 41**
8th Key | **Stay Perfectly Focused on God's Word 45**
9th Key | **Allow the Anointing to Flow into Your Mind 54**
10th Key | **Let God be Your Strength 63**
11th Key | **Pray in the Spirit 71**
12th Key | **Fear God 74**
13th Key | **Clean Up! 79**
14th Key | **Shun Worldliness 85**
15th Key | **Humbly Accept God's Word 89**
16th Key | **Seek God's Ways 96**
17th Key | **Be Merciful 102**
18th Key | **Mind Your Own Business 106**
19th Key | **Go For Prophetic Plans 119**

1st Key

Develop an Open and Hearing Ear

How terrifying it must have been for Moses as he faced the Red Sea with over two million Israelites.[1] Their enemies were hot in pursuit from behind, while they were hopelessly hedged in between two mountains, completely trapped, and at the mercy of the Egyptians.

I'd like you to imagine for a moment that you were Moses, and that you had called a meeting of the other leaders to figure out how to deal with the situation.

What kinds of suggestions and solutions do you think you and your leaders would have brought forward?

I bet you'll think along the lines of building rafters, negotiating with Pharaoh and his army, or maybe everyman for himself.

In any case, I seriously doubt that any of your leaders would have suggested that you stretch out a stick over the sea to part it into two!

---

[1] Exodus 14:5-31

Yet, that was exactly what Moses did![1]

Now, that's what I refer to as an *uncommon solution.*

An uncommon solution is simply that; uncommon, unconventional, unimaginable.

During an extensive and intensive spiritual and faith-building program, which included fifty four days of fasting, praying, prophetic utterances, midnight vigils, spiritual warfare, and so on, God unfolded to me the mystery of 'uncommon solutions.'

This book contains a lot of what He showed me during that period.

As you will discover in the pages of this book, uncommon solutions are actually what we term miracles and are within our reach if only we can connect to the frequency of God.

Uncommon solutions are those mysterious highways provided by God through the Red Seas of life. They are supernatural highways to realizing your dreams.

Here's another scenario.

---

[1] Exodus 14:27-28

At a wedding event in Cana, they ran out of drinks. Jesus and His mum were present. So, Mary, His mother approached Him for help.[1]

Again, imagine the number of options you'd have come up with. I'm absolutely certain you would never have imagined Jesus' solution.

"Nearby stood six stone water jars, the kind used by the Jews for ceremonial washing, each holding from twenty to thirty gallons. Jesus said to the servants "Fill the jars with water"; so they filled them to the brim.

Then he told them, "Now draw some out and take it to the master of the banquet." They did so, and the master of the banquet tasted the water that had been turned into wine."[2]

He turned water into wine!

That's what I call an uncommon solution.

Fill the jars with water, draw some out and take it to the master of the banquet.

What a solution!

_____

[1] John 2:1-11
[2] John 2:5-10

An uncommon solution is that mysterious, strange, supernatural, and divine idea whose execution delivers phenomenal results to you!

Note that the solution came from Jesus Christ. He created the 'idea'. Such is the nature of uncommon solutions. They are God's ideas, God's thoughts; they come from God.

Notice again that it was the servants that executed this uncommon solution. They didn't create it, Jesus did; but they executed it, and subsequently manifested its results.

So, whereas God may plant uncommon solutions as divine ideas within your mind, it will often require your obedience, including the use of your efforts, to execute that solution and manifest its results.

Now, observe how Mary prepared the grounds for the turning of water into wine by telling the servants there to, "Do whatever he tells you."

The very nature of uncommon solutions dictates that you cannot manifest them in your life unless you do *whatever God tells you*. And this can only happen if He wakens and opens your ears to hear His voice.

Whether you turn to the right or to the left, your ears will hear a voice behind you, saying "This is the way; walk in it."[1]

"He wakens me morning by morning, wakens my ear to listen like one being taught. The Sovereign Lord has opened my ears, and I have not been rebellious; I have not drawn back."[2]

The ultimate secret to uncommon solutions is your ability to hear God's voice within you.

Uncommon solutions are created by God in the realms of the spirit and then manifested on earth by individuals who can hear and obey His voice.

When your inner ears *can hear* God's voice, uncommon solutions and manifestations will characterize your life.

"The entrance of thy words giveth light; it giveth understanding unto the simple."[3]

When His living voice penetrates your ears, and saturates your mind, it creates light within. This light is the wisdom of God Himself. It is through this entrance of His voice, through your inner ears, that your head becomes anointed

---

[1] Isaiah 30:21
[2] Isaiah 50:4,5
[3] Psalm 119:130

with oil. His voice in your mind is the essence of the anointing of your head, which creates abundance and overflow in your life.

"...You anoint my head with oil; my cup overflows."[1]

In contrast, when your ears cannot hear His voice, you experience a closed or dead mind - one that is devoid of supernatural ideas and divine signals. This is why many religious people's lives are so colourless and empty of divine manifestations. Their ears and minds are shut tight.

Here are some keys to developing an open and hearing ear.

#1: Focus on pleasing God

If your focus is on how to please God, and your mind becomes fixated on that, His voice will penetrate your heart easily.[2]

An open mind is one that is focused on how to make God happy.

---

[1] Psalm 23:5
[2] Romans 8:5-8

A carnal mind, on the other hand, being self-centred, shuts off the mind from God's reach. Actually, another word for carnality is selfishness, and selfishness shuts the mind.

Spirituality and carnality refer to your mindset, that is, the orientation, and inclination of your mind. They talk about your dominant mental preoccupations.

If your mind is centred on what your flesh wants, it will inevitably become closed off to God's voice.

Get your mind set today on how to please God and make Him happy. Then watch out as divine ideas flood your mind.

#2: Get intimate with the Holy Spirit

To be 'without the Spirit'[1] means that one is not in the Holy Spirit's inner circle; that is to say, not intimate with Him.

When you are intimate with the Holy Spirit He opens your mind and shows you mysterious secrets to success that are not commonly available.

---

[1] 1 Corinthians 2:14

#3: Get quiet before the Lord

Until you get still before Him you won't 'know'.[1]

One very powerful way to achieve this spiritual stillness is to engage in sustained seasons and sessions of praying and fasting.

Then boost your fasting and prayers with solitude and inspirational materials such as the bible and the inspirational writings, and messages of anointed men and women of God.

When you separate yourself and get alone with God, the scriptures, and anointed materials, His voice will easily penetrate your mind.

Now may the Lord waken your ears to hear. May He strengthen your heart and resolve to do whatever He tells you. And may your life become abundantly decorated with uncommon solutions, as you continue to read this book, in the name of Jesus Christ.

Amen.

---

[1] Psalm 46:10

2nd Key

Eliminate Every Hindrance to Hearing God's Voice

The possibilities of God are limitless, and you can tap into His unsearchable reservoir of uncommon solutions simply by believing and acting on His instructions. This is the central teaching of this book.

When you hear God's voice, and you act on it, it is called *faith*. And when you act on God's instructions, powerful manifestations occur.

Faith is acting on God's instructions. You hear His command in your heart, then you act on it; that acting on it is faith.[1]

So, faith can neither exist nor work without God's instructions and commands.

And, as I strongly emphasized in the first chapter, you cannot receive divine instructions and commands if your ears can neither hear nor recognize God's voice.

---

[1] Romans 10:17

There are various reasons people cannot hear the living voice of God. I've listed some of them below in the hope that by eliminating these hindrances, your heart will become better conditioned to hear God's voice and receive His instructions.

#1: Ignorance of the scriptures[1]

It is very difficult for a heart that is empty of God's written words to hear His spoken words.

To enhance your spiritual hearing, spend more time meditating on the Scriptures.

#2. Disobedience to the written word of God

Jesus Christ says, "If anyone chooses to do God's will, he will find out whether my teaching comes from God or whether I speak on my own."[2]

He that chooses to DO God's will, *will find out...*

It is very difficult to hear the voice of God when you are living in disobedience to God's written commandments and instructions. Why would God speak to you if you are

---

[1] Mark 12:24; Deuteronomy 29:29; Colossians 3:16
[2] John 7:17

consciously ignoring stuff He'd already said to you in His word?

Got it?

Sin in the heart blocks the voice of God.

#3: Worldliness and the cares of this world[1]

It is hard for an anxious heart to hear God.

When your heart and mind are filled with worldly and carnal desires, with your own interests and concerns, it is very difficult to hear the voice of God.

If you want to hear God's voice, you must learn to shut out the noise of earthly cares through fasting, solitude, and bible meditations.

#4: Unfamiliarity with God's voice

Now Samuel did not yet know the Lord: The word of the Lord had not yet been revealed to him.[2]

---

[1] Psalm 46:10; Isaiah 30:15
[2] 1 Samuel 3:7

Samuel's problem here wasn't that of *hearing*, but rather that of *recognition*. He could hear the voice but had no idea who was speaking because He had not yet known the Lord.

Unfamiliarity with God's voice can be due to failure to spend quality time with Him, with His word, and with those who know Him. So even when he speaks, like Samuel, you are not able to recognize His voice.

I remember sometime ago, when my daughter was just about 4 years old. She ran out to the sitting room where I was sitting screaming excitedly, "Auntie so and so is coming."

A group of people had just entered our compound and you could hear their voices as they chatted. Yes, I could hear the voice of the auntie she was referring to, but I was curious as to how my little girl knew the auntie in question was among those approaching.

So, I asked her, "Are you absolutely certain it's auntie so and so?"

She responded with a very confident "Yes!"

To which I replied, "But you cannot see her. So how are you certain she's the one?"

She replied matter-of-factly, "I know her *sound*."

Well, there you have it: *I know her sound...*

And she was absolutely right!

Many people have asked me over the years, "How do you know that this is God's voice?" And, in the words of my four year old daughter, I always respond, "I'm certain because I know His *sound.*"

I cannot teach you how to hear and recognize God's voice anymore than my little girl could have taught me how to recognize that auntie's voice.

But this one thing I know: The more time you spend in worship, in prayers, in the scriptures, and in the company of men and women of God, the more you are able to hear and recognize God's voice.

Remember, as I showed you in Chapter one, that the ultimate secret to uncommon solutions is the ability to hear God's voice within you. And just as you learnt there to develop an open and hearing ear, it is also important to eliminate every hindrance to hearing God's voice from your life.

3rd Key

Strengthen Your Faith in God

A piece of ancient prophecy declares that the people who survive the sword will find favour in the desert.[1]

The sword speaks of calamities, adversities, and storms, and I can tell you with every certainty that tough times are ahead. There are stormy weathers up front.

You think this world has known trouble?
Wait till you see what's coming.

However, even in the desert, there is favour!

Favour in the desert refers to the uncommon solutions of the Almighty God. It refers to His supernatural provisions even in the worst of times and circumstances. It is a beautiful description of the limitless possibilities of God.

This *favour in the desert*, however, is only accessible to those who *survive the sword*, that is, those who outlast the storms of life. Favour in the desert is for those who,

---

[1] Jeremiah 31:2

according to Jesus Christ, have built their houses on the Rock.[1]

As a matter of fact, waves of adversities also offer great opportunities for blessings, favour, and distinction for those who have built their houses on the Rock!

To build your house on the Rock means to focus on strengthening your faith in God, and deepening your spiritual roots in Him. There's really no other alternative if you want to survive the sword and find favour in the desert.[2]

I pray you are listed among those who *find favour in the desert.* While others are groaning in despair and despondency, while all around is dryness and famine, you will be distinguished by the favour of the Lord!

A powerful key to unlocking this favour, is to *please God. Without faith it's impossible to please God,*[3] meaning that your faith is the central key to pleasing God. Therefore, it is vital for you to strengthen your faith in God.

---

[1] Matthew 7:24,25
[2] Jeremiah 31:2
[3] Hebrews 11:6

Your faith is the key to experiencing impossibilities, for all things are possible to him that believes.[1]

Unless you take the time to strengthen your faith in God and deepen your spiritual roots in Him, you will find yourself labouring in vain.[2]

You should never toil in vain.

You see, everything does not always answer to efforts. It is possible to struggle and labour in vain, that is *efforts without results;* which, by the way, is the plight of many today.

Have you ever tried, and in spite of all your efforts, failed to make things work? I bet you'll agree with me when I say that success is not entirely a matter of efforts. It's rather more about God's grace and favour.

You need the grace and favour of God in your life, else you will labour and toil in vain; that is not God's plan for you. He grants sleep – that is, *rest, ease, comfort, success without stress* - to those He loves!

So, there's no need for you to toil in the flesh without results. You should never labour in vain; you don't have to.

---

[1] Mark 9:23
[2] Psalm 127:1-2

Just strengthen your faith in God and deepen your roots in Him. Let Him build your house; let Him watch over your city, and, yes, let Him give you sleep.

At this time, I challenge you to focus on developing certain core spiritual disciplines. These spiritual disciplines are also spiritual strategies, weapons, and tools.

Life is essentially spiritual.

Miracles and uncommon solutions do not reside in the natural realm. They reside in the spiritual realms; when you activate them there, things begin to change in the natural.

It is far better to labour in the spirit and rest in the body, than to slumber in the spirit and struggle in the flesh.

I encourage you to focus on strengthening your faith by developing the core spiritual disciplines of *daily bible study and meditation*, *praying*, *fasting*, and *sacrificial giving*.

As I said already, these are spiritual disciplines as well as spiritual strategies, weapons, and tools.

In order to strengthen your faith in God, you must establish yourself in these spiritual disciplines. This will allow you to know who you are in Him, what He expects from you, and what He has said concerning you.

And more importantly, you will be able to withstand the storms of life, survive the sword, and ultimately find favour in the desert.

A strong faith is your access to the limitless possibilities of God's uncommon solutions.

4ᵗʰ Key

Utilize the Spiritual Weapons of Praying and Fasting

One of the reasons many Christians live sub-normal lives, oppressed, and harassed by Satan is because they are too lazy to fast.[1]

Numerous examples from the bible, plus the experiences of God's children down through the ages, demonstrate that you can turn the tides of life in your favour by using the spiritual weapons of praying and fasting.

Yes, *praying and fasting* are powerful keys for gaining access to the mysterious and powerful solutions that our Almighty God has for us. Uncommon solutions and supernatural manifestations abound in the lives of men and women who pray and fast regularly.

The story of Esther in the bible is a classic illustration of what can happen when we fast and pray.[2]

---

[1] Matthew 17:21
[2] Esther 4:9-16

Because Esther fasted and prayed, the law was changed on her behalf and favour was unloaded upon her. She used the weapon of fasting to turn the tables against her enemies.

You too can turn the tables of life in your favour by using the spiritual weapons of praying and fasting.

Just as Esther got the law changed in her favour, you also can reverse every contrary law in your destiny in your favour.

By laws, I mean traditions, perceptions, policies, institutions, and regulations. They could be physical, biological, political, cultural, religious, or economic.

I see every law that is against you changed in your favour!

By the way, Jesus Christ has already cancelled every written code against you in the spirit[1]

Again, because Esther and the Jews fasted and prayed, the Persian king stretched out the royal sceptre of favour toward her, thereby placing all his power, resources, and influence at her disposal.

In the same manner, as I write, I can see powerful and influential hands - kings and mighty men - stretched out to

---

[1] Colossians 2:13-15

favour you as you cultivate the powerful spiritual disciplines of praying and fasting.[1]

Praying and fasting are spiritual tools for flushing out stubborn demons and spiritual poisons.[2]

A lot of people are suffering from the oppressions of demon spirits and spiritual poisons in their lives, health, marriages, finances, families, and so on.

Here's a list of some of the manifestations of spiritual poisons: *Besetting sins, mysterious diseases, spiritual weakness, demonic sleep, false friends - wolves in sheep clothing, bad dreams, spiritual blindness and deafness.*

Spiritual poisons enter through sin;[3] sin is the sting of death.

So, take a brief pause from your reading to ask God to forgive you every known and unknown sin in your life, then plead the blood of Jesus Christ over your life.

Now, it is time to get on with the business of praying and fasting.

---

[1] Isaiah 60:10-12
[2] Matthew 17:21
[3] John 5:13, 14; 1 Corinthians 15:56.

Boldly make the following prophetic declarations of deliverance over your life right away.

Every spirit that has degraded, disgraced, and robbed me of my dignity is under Holy Ghost arrest right now!

Every situation that has harassed me is under divine arrest right now!

Every force that has tormented my life is under arrest right now!

Every stubborn spirit of disease that has sickened my body is under arrest right now!

Every covenant with all evil spiritual husbands and wives is forever broken right now!

Every satanic mountains and demonic blockades on my way is destroyed right now!

Every wicked serpent of stagnation that has coiled around my life is under arrest right now!

One of the blessings I pray for you as you read this book is that you'll contact a strong anointing and unction for fervency in praying and fasting.

5th Key

Put Your Foot Down!

The number one reward for a season of fasting and praying is divine revelation. Whenever you set time apart to seek God in praying and fasting, you should expect spiritual and prophetic insight into God's promises for you and other people.

This is why I seriously emphasize bible reading and meditations during any season of fasting.

As you continue in your journey through the pages of this book, I pray that God gives you deeper spiritual insight into your destiny and those of the people you care about.

Now take a moment's break and pray this Psalm:

"Open thou mine eyes, that I may behold wondrous things out of thy law." [1]

Victorious and effective praying is usually the offspring of spiritual and prophetic insight into God's promises for you and other people.

---

[1] Psalm 119:18

This was the case with Daniel. During a time of fasting, praying, and meditation, he gained deep spiritual and prophetic insight from the scriptures regarding God's promises for his people.[1]

This understanding then led him to pray one of the most effectual and victorious prayers recorded in the bible.[2]

Daniel's powerful and effective prayer also reveals certain vital elements of the kind of prayer that works. These elements include: *Praise and adoration*, *humble and sincere repentance*, u*nselfish intercession, Scripture-based supplications and petitions.*

At the heart of my message to you in this book is a call to a life of praying and fasting, because *praying and fasting* are powerful keys for gaining access to the mysterious and powerful solutions that our Almighty God has for us. Uncommon solutions and supernatural manifestations abound in the lives of men and women who pray and fast regularly.

I pray, in accordance with Zechariah 12:10, that God may pour upon you the spirit of grace and supplication.

---

[1] Daniel 9
[2] Daniel 9:4-19

Another very powerful result of praying and fasting is the ministration of angels. This is also seen in the case of Daniel. In response to his praying and fasting, an angel came to him in swift flight, bringing a message, instructions, insight, understanding, and vision.[1]

As a result of his praying and fasting, Daniel obtained divine revelation and gained supernatural insight into the destiny of his people through the ministrations of angels. This is what happens when you pray effectually and victoriously.

I pray that the Lord may grant you angelic visitations and divine revelations regarding your destiny at this time.

Certain individuals have shaped the destinies of nations and influenced the course of human history through effectual and victorious praying. Daniel is unquestionably one of them. He was a man of tremendous power in prayer.

His prayer power stands in sharp contrast to the lip-gloss, drive-in, microwave type that is so widespread in today's Christianity.

Daniel's prayer was that effectual, fervent, and prevailing prayer of a righteous man that avails much in its

---

[1] Daniel 9:20-23; Hebrews 1:14

workings.[1] His prayer here[2] is an example of what I call power praying - a high-intensity spiritual force that goes all out to break barriers and obtain the desired results.

I challenge you to learn to add prolonged and sustained fasting to your prayer arsenal. This is because that kind of fasting is a prayer power booster!

The manifestation of God's answers to your prayers will be resisted by the kingdom of darkness. Satan and his evil cohorts will use every trick in the book to frustrate your results.[3] This is no myth. For this reason, half-hearted and lazy praying will get you nowhere. You might as well be playing possum, in the blind hope that somehow things will turn out right for you.

I'd rather take hold of God's power and authority in prayer, root out every spiritual opposition, and possess my possessions!

This was exactly what Daniel did.

He held on for three weeks in persistent and importunate fasting and praying until all spiritual resistance caved in.[4]

---

[1] James 5:16b
[2] Daniel 10:2, 3
[3] Daniel 10:12, 13

[4] Daniel 10:12-14

As I write, I can sense some high-level strategic spiritual resistance to the manifestations of answers to your prayers. Therefore put your foot down in fasting, praying, and vigils until all oppositions melt.

6th Key

Expect Waves Of Favours!

When three powerful nations ganged up against the people of Israel during the reign of Jehoshaphat, their attack triggered off a mighty manifestation of the Holy Spirit.

Jehoshaphat called the entire nation to prayer to seek God's help in response to this threat.

"Then the Spirit of the Lord came upon Jahaziel son of Zechariah, the son of Benaiah, the son of Jeiel, the son of Mattaniah, a Levite and descendant of Asaph, as he stood in the assembly."[1]

The results of this manifestation of the Holy Spirit were massive waves of favours that began with the total annihilation of their enemies, and ended with such a release of abundance that took the entire nation three days to gather the plunder.[2]

---

[1] 2 Chronicles 20:14
[2] 2 Chronicles 20:22-25

Waves of favours are God's uncommon solutions unleashed in your life when the *Holy Spirit* manifests aggressively on your behalf to confound your enemies and glorify God in your life.

Waves of Favours are essentially the various consequences of the aggressive manifestations of *God's Holy Spirit* in your life.

Few things trigger these manifestations as much as attacks from your enemies. So, do not panic when people gang up against you to attack you in any way. In fact, get excited because you are right then at the threshold of *waves of favours!*

Let me share this secret with you; the attacks of your enemies are triggers for the manifestations of the *Holy Spirit* in your life!

The enemy boasted, 'I will pursue, I will overtake them. I will divide the spoils; I will gorge myself on them. I will draw my sword and my hand will destroy them. But you blew with your breath, and the sea covered them. They sank like lead in the mighty waters."[1]

The breath of God here refers to *His Spirit*.

---

[1] Exodus 15:9,10

Every time the enemy comes at you, the attack automatically triggers off an aggressive move of the *Holy Spirit*. This move then releases the following extraordinary manifestations in your life: Unlocking of uncommon solutions for you, execution of the Lord's vengeance upon your enemies, and access to divine favours.

"So shall they fear the name of the Lord from the west, and his glory from the rising of the sun. When the enemy shall come in, like a flood, the Spirit of the Lord shall lift up a standard against him."[1]

You must, however, seek God's help *first*, just as Jehoshaphat and the Israelites did.

"And call on me in the day of trouble; I will deliver you, and you will honour me."[2]

I challenge you to trust God for the following five remarkable manifestations of God's glorious waves of favours in your life: The dismantling of spiritual wickedness in your life, termination of evil and wicked activities of hidden enemies, permanent driving out of the demonic forces that have been operating in your life, speedy

---

[1] Isaiah 59:19
[2] Psalm 50:15

springing forth of your health, and release of supernatural access to wealth.

Now pray, "Oh Lord, let your waves of favours rain on me now!"

7th Key

Operate God's Faith

"...there is the sound of a heavy rain..." [1]

What sounds can you hear? What sights and visions do you see?

It's time you stopped watching the physical winds of negative circumstances. Stop listening to the sounds of your fears, doubts, and worries.

Instead, listen attentively to God's Spirit within you for *the sound of a heavy rain*.

If you've been spending time in God's word, if you understand His perfect will for you, and have established your heart in it, hearing this sound of a heavy rain would not be difficult. [2]

Rain depicts a new season. It signifies the end of the dry spell that has been cast over you by the enemy. It

---

[1] 1Kings 18:41
[2] Psalm 112:7-8

symbolizes abundance, blessings, and divine favours. Rain represents a time of renewal and refreshing from the presence of the Lord.

There is nothing in creation that suggests that God ever wanted us to just get by. Instead, all we see around us clearly show that God's default for us is abundance; He has richly provided us with everything for our enjoyment.[1]

Be sensitive to the ebb and flow of God's Holy Spirit within you. The Almighty Creator of this extravagantly abundant universe is mightily at work within you.[2]

The level of spiritual sensitivity required to tune in to this power, however, is impossible if your mind is noisy and distracted. A noisy mind is toxic to abundance. For this reason, you must learn to cultivate inner quietness, serenity, and tranquility.[3]

Those who master the spiritual disciplines of inner solitude and quietness, experience a dimension of abundance that others never quite comprehend.[4]

---

[1] 1 Timothy 6:17
[2] Ephesians 3:20
[3] 1 Thessalonians 4:11
[4] Genesis 24:63

Tune in to the living and pulsating vibrations, signals, and words of God's eternal Spirit within you.

As I have continued to emphasize in this book, faith is a powerful key to enjoying God's uncommon solutions. And the faith I speak of in this book is none other than God's faith that comes from hearing God's voice.

If you can listen attentively to God's Spirit within you, and if you can hear this sound of a heavy rain that I speak of, you will become empowered to operate God's faith.

God's faith operates through speaking. God sees what He wants, and then He speaks it into being.[1] That is God's faith, and that is the kind of faith that moves your life forward.

God's faith is essential to spiritual progress and personal success.[2] Every time you stop operating God's faith, your life becomes stagnant and automatically triggers a downward spiral of lack and more lack.

To operate God's faith, use the greatest power that God has placed in you – your tongue.[3] You have in your mouth, the power to arrest and direct your thoughts.

---

[1] Genesis 1:3
[2] Hebrews 10:38
[3] Proverbs 18:21; James 3:1-12

Now listen…

Can you hear the sound of a heavy rain? Can you feel it? Can you sense it pulsating within your spirit?

Then vocalize and verbalize what you hear; give it expression to recreate and release abundance in your life.

8th Key

Stay Perfectly Focused on God's Word

Recently, during one my personal meditation times, the Lord gave me these words regarding His children:

"Oh my child, if only you knew how much you lose daily by operating in the flesh like the rest of the world. Learn to spend more time with me, for a day in my courts is far more rewarding than a thousand elsewhere."[1]

"I can do more for you in a minute," He continued, "than anything you could ever achieve for yourself in ten years."

"Surrender everything to Me, and let Me have My way in your life."

"Stop minding the distractions of the media and earthly circumstances, for it is time to start operating in the frequency of the god that you are."

There is a call at this hour from God for you to strengthen your focus on His Word. Each day, hour by hour, and

---

[1] Psalm 84:10

moment by moment, you must keep your heart and mind glued to God's words. This is so that you can walk by the spirit and not gratify the desires of the flesh.[1]

Satan understands the power of God's words, and that of a life that is operating by the spirit of God's voice. His primary strategy, therefore, is to disconnect you from God's words, and keep you perpetually distracted by the things of this life.

Your fellowship with God and your meditations on the revelations of His words are key targets of Satan.

More so, his main tool for breaking your focus is *busyness with the things of the world.* He gets you busy with the things of this world and then pollutes your mindset with that of this world. The result is that your mind becomes hostile to God, and unable to appreciate His ways.[2]

Satan's strategy of distraction is two-pronged:

First, he intensifies the cares and burdens of this present life upon your mind, thus increasing the challenges and struggles of your earthly existence.

---

[1] Galatians 5:16
[2] Romans 8:7

Secondly, he paints a picture of God's words as impotent, ineffective, and false.

His ultimate goal in all this is to dominate your life, and keep you perpetually threading the mill of slavery and frustration.

Carefully observe how Satan implemented his wicked strategy of distraction against the people of Israel when Moses arrived with God's word to deliver them from the bondage of Pharaoh.[1] Pay particular attention to Pharaoh's statement, "Make the work harder for the people so that they keep working and pay no attention to lies."[2]

The encounter between Moses and Pharaoh epitomizes the conflict between the Children of God and the world. Israel here is a type of the people of God, Egypt represents the world, while Pharaoh symbolizes Satan - the prince and mastermind of the evil world system.

Once again, note the two prongs of his evil strategy: First, he intensified their cares and burdens by demanding that they make bricks without straw;[3] then, he represented

---

[1] Exodus 5:1-9
[2] Exodus 5:9
[3] Exodus 5:6-8

God's words as lies! His ultimate goal in all this was to keep them threading the mill of slavery and frustration.

Why is the devil so threatened by our focus on God's words? Well, in a nutshell, it's because the words of God are absolutely powerful!

#1: God's words make you wise[1]

Satan, your ultimate enemy, knows too well the truth that God's words make you wiser than he is.

When you are focused on God's words, and are walking by them, you will constantly outwit that cunning serpent.

Satan is threatened by your focus on God's words, because they place you beyond the range of his wiles and devices.

God's words are able to make you wise for salvation. For that reason, do not let anything distract you from God's words. Stay tuned to His voice and never disconnect.

#2: God's words build you up and give you an inheritance.[2]

Yes, God's words can build you up. They reinforce and strengthen you to thrive in all locations and occasions.

---

[1] Psalm 119: 97,98; 2 Timothy 3:15
[2] Acts 20:32

God's words enlarge you and make you a force to reckon with on the earth. This is a clear threat to the devil; so he will do all he can to break your focus on the Word.

God's words also give you an inheritance. This means that by the words of God, you are connected to His resources, His assets, and His wealth.

Meditate on this truth for a while: *by God's words you get connected.*

God's words give you an inheritance, thereby exempting you from the necessity of sweating and struggling to make it in life.

Beloved, don't let Satan rob you of your glorious inheritance. Stay tuned and focused on God's words.

#3: God's words make you a wonder to the powers of darkness.[1]

The light and life of God's words are incomprehensible and unconquerable to the world!

It is easy for Satan to comprehend, predict, and control people who walk in the natural. When you operate by your natural senses and mere human logic, you are a cheap

---

[1] John 1:4, 5

prey for Satan; but, when you operate by the wisdom, counsel, and power of God's words, you become a mystery and wonder to the forces of darkness.

Satan cannot handle men and women of God's words!

#4: God's words transform you into the likeness of Jesus Christ.[1]

You become what you behold - the more you meditate on God's words, the more you literally metamorphose into the nature and power of Jesus Christ.

Oh, how the devil hates that! It rattles that old rattle snake!

When you ignore Satan's tricks and distractions, and focus on God's words, you are transformed into the likeness of Jesus Christ with ever-increasing glory.

Praise God!

God's words transform you into the likeness of Jesus Christ with ever-increasing glory.

In 1 Peter 1:4, we read that God's words make you a partaker of God's own nature, and put you beyond the range of this world's decay.

---

[1] 2 Corinthians 3:18

Satan's trick against the Israelites in Exodus 5:9 was to keep them busy with work and more work. He is using the same trick today, keeping God's children hustling and bustling to no end, achieving absolutely nothing.

God created work, of course, but it is one thing to be employed by God, and another to be employed by Satan, the prince of this world.

According to Proverbs 14:23, "in all labour there is profit." The question, however, is 'who is getting that profit or reward - you or your slave master?' Is it the kingdom of God that is profiting from your efforts, or that of Satan?

You see, there are basically two kinds of labour:

First, there is the kind that intensifies your bondage to the systems of this world. This kind of labour enriches Pharaoh and Egypt. It makes you a part of the rat race. It makes you a victim.

Then, there is the kind that frees you. This kind enriches you eternally. It makes you a winner and leads you to rest.[1] Paying attention to God's word and fellowshipping with Him falls into this second kind of labour.

---

[1] Hebrews 4:11

My point here is that you should not allow the challenges of life, and the demands of day-to-day living, distract you from God and His words. Don't become too busy to meditate on the word of God and fellowship with Him.[1]

Just as the word was given to the Israelites through Moses, the word has been given to you today. You need to pay attention to it.

It is one thing to receive the word into your heart by reading, hearing, and so on. It is another thing to pay continuous and undistracted attention to it.

You see, the discipline of remaining focused on the Word and being intimate with the Lord in a chaotic world is an uphill task. It is work. It requires effort. It demands a fight and great resistance. However, it is a labour that leads to great rest, great reward, and great favour.

Devote yourself to prayer, worship, and the word. A daily bible devotional is a good idea. Just ensure that each day, you read and meditate on a portion of God's word to discover yourself in Him.

Stop minding the distractions of the market, the media, and other earthly illusions.

---

[1] 2 Peter 1:19; Hebrews 2:1

Separate at least one day in a month for solitude, praying, and fasting, as well as for studying the word of God.

If you master this discipline of staying perfectly focused on God's Word, then every other thing that others hustle and bustle to get will fall head-over-heels to get at you.

9th Key

Allow the Anointing to Flow into Your Mind

As I write this chapter, I can sense deep within my spirit that something great is about to happen in your life. I can feel it so strongly that my entire being is electrified with excitement. It is hard to describe this in human terms, because it's really *huge.*

The floodgates of Heaven are open for you.

Something phenomenal is about to happen within you that will change everything. I can feel the burbling of overflowing joy.

God is raising you to a completely new level. He has been preparing you, and setting you up for this. He is bringing you to a dimension where nothing can stop you, and where nothing will be impossible for you.

Rejoice, for you are about to soar to new heights that you have never reached before, and move at speeds you have never attained before. I just know it.

Now is the time. Yes, the floodgates of Heaven are open for you.

Gates of opportunities and favours have been unlocked for you.

The magnetism of divinity has been installed within you.

Alleluia!

I see multitudes coming to you, drawn by the majestic display of God's favours on your life.

A time of great ease has come; you will no longer need to struggle to achieve God's results.

So far, you may have been struggling and wading in shallow waters, but now He is moving you into the deepest depths where you cannot even swim anymore. You will rather be carried along by the flood of His supernatural power.

This flood of divine glory and favour cannot be contained; it is welling up and overflowing for your lifting and glory.

"He measured off another thousand, *but now it was a river that I could not cross because the water had risen and was deep enough to swim in* – a river that no one could cross."[1]

Hallelujah! The dams have broken, and the floodgates of Heaven are open for you!

---

[1] Ezekiel 47:6

Now, you shall be swept off by the current.

Satan and the powers of darkness are no match for this.

This is mighty, it is awesome, it is from the Lord, and it cannot be contained.

"When I arrived there *I saw a great number of trees* on each side of the river."[1]

Trees represent *people;* so, this is a season of great increase, as multitudes are drawn to you.

Trees also represent *prosperity.* Therefore, this also will be a season of great prosperity, as resources are drawn to you.

Thank You Lord.

"He said to me, 'This water flows toward the eastern region and goes down into the Arabah, *where it enters the sea, the water there becomes fresh*'"[2]

Reflect on this: *Where it enters the sea, the water there becomes fresh.*

This is talking about the flood of life - the *life-giving* force – that has been released upon you. Consequently, dead

---

[1] Ezekiel 47:7
[2] Ezekiel 47:8

things are coming alive in you and in your circumstances; stolen and lost things are being restored.

This is your season of refreshing: Fatigue gives way to faith, and weakness gives way to strength.

Yes, you are coming alive, and everything within you is being revitalized with new power and new force!

Amen. Glory to God!

Sea speaks of *multitudes,* but it also speaks of *deadness*.

Thus, this anointing will cause the *sea* of tired, dead, lost, broken, battered, and barren old things in your life, to become *fresh waters* of vital, living, important, strong, refreshed, fruitful, glorious, and productive new you.

Imagine a *sea* turning into a *river!* This is metamorphosis, and nothing is impossible with God.

Your season of transformation is here. Nothing like it has ever been, and all that see you, will know that it could only have been orchestrated by God.

"Swarms of living creatures will live wherever the river flows. There will be large numbers of fish, because this water flows there and makes the salt water fresh; *so where the river flows everything will live*"[1]

Observe that it is all 'because this *river* flows there'.

Just think about it.

I thank You Lord for this *river*.

Beloved, the flow has already started; nothing can stop it. It is overflowing, and cannot be contained.

"Fruit trees of all kinds will grow on both banks of the river. Their leaves will not wither, nor will their fruit fail. Every month they will bear, *because the water from the sanctuary flows to them.* Their fruit will serve for food and their leaves will be for healing."[2]

Do not miss the point here, which is that you will experience all of these diverse uncommon solutions *because* of the water flowing from the sanctuary - a prophetic reference to the presence and power of God.

Now, ponder on this: Paul planted and Apollos watered, but the Lord made it to grow and increase.[3]

---

[1] Ezekiel 47:9
[2] Ezekiel 47:12
[3] 1 Corinthians 3:6-7

Human planting and watering are nothing but efforts, efforts, and more efforts. All our efforts mean nothing apart from the Lord, for He is the One that *gives the increase*.

Now God's Spirit has begun to move. The *water from the sanctuary* has begun to flow into your life.

Behold, fruit trees of all kinds are beginning to grow on both banks of the river.

Your leaves will never wither, nor will your fruits ever fail!

Your fruit will serve for food. Multitudes will be fed and blessed from the prosperity, favour, blessing, and increase that the Lord is now bestowing upon you.

Your leaves will serve for healing. This is a description of the level of influence, relevance, and significance that you will begin to enjoy from now on.

Nations will come to you for nourishment, and the peoples for healing, because your hour of glory has come.

Therefore, let your expectations loose, and let your imagination soar to new heights.

The floodgates of Heaven are open, the dams are broken, and the river is overflowing unto you.

Our God is mighty, and He is about to show your enemies *how mighty He really is.*

Also, because He is fed up with your trying to do it in human energy, He has come to take over the affairs of your life. He has a lot to do and does not want you to waste His time, or mess up His work. For this reason, He has decided to burst through the dams and invade your life!

Prosperity grows wherever the anointing flows. Put in another way, wealth follows the anointing.

As a matter of fact, from Luke 4:16-21, it is clear that the very first evil targeted by Jesus' anointing was poverty.

When your head is anointed, your cup begins to overflow.[1] This means that overflow – that is, abundance, or prosperity – is a principal outcome of the anointing.

However, this prosperity happens only when you allow the anointing to flow into your life, and your finances.

Study Ezekiel 47:1-12, and carefully mark the ninth verse, particularly the phrase, '*where the river flows, everything*

---

[1] Psalm 23:5

will live,' because the anointing will produce only where you let Him.

From the above text, we know where the anointing originates from. The issue, however, is *where will you channel the flow?*

The anointing flows from God's temple, that is, from within you – a reference to the spiritual dimension of your being. Then, according to the text above, He empties into the Dead Sea which signifies your natural dimension.

God's Anointing, therefore, will not produce as long as He is confined to the spiritual sphere of your being. He has to flow out of *the temple* of your spirit into *the sea* of your mind. It is in the latter that *He inspires, instructs, guides, and controls your words, decisions, choices, and actions.* Here, He tells you exactly what to do, transforming lofty prophecies into specific ideas and instructions that can be applied as uncommon solutions to real-life problems.

This is what it means to have your head anointed with oil; you are *being led* by the Holy Spirit, instead of just *being filled* with Him.

Understand that it is not those who are *filled with* the Holy Spirit that are the sons of God; it is those who are *led by* Him.[1]

To have your head anointed with oil, that is, to have the river flow from the temple into the Dead Sea, means that the anointing you have received is now teaching and counselling you.

As for you, the anointing you received from him remains in you, and you do not need anyone to teach you. But as his anointing teaches you about all things and as that anointing is real, not counterfeit – just as it has taught you, remain in him.[2]

Just as He came in when you simply asked Him to, it is time to ask Him, "Lord, what must I do?" Then listen carefully.

Let Him have His way in your life. Let go. Surrender all!

Now go and meditate on what you have received. Also share this great news with your loved ones.

---

[1] Romans 8:14
[2] 1 John 2:27

10th Key

Let God be Your Strength

...for by strength shall no man prevail[1]

The core message of this book is not just that the possibilities of God are infinitely limitless, but also that you can draw from His unsearchable reservoir of uncommon solutions for your every need.

First of all, however, you must humbly acknowledge Him in all your ways[2]; and so cease from your own struggles. None of us is strong, or smart enough to make it on our own. We all need the help of God to take us into the Promised Land, and to possess God's promises to us.

I am absolutely convinced in the Lord that, in spite of all your weaknesses, and against all odds, you will fulfil your destiny - that is, as long as you look up to the Lord and depend on His help rather than on your own strength.[3]

---

[1] 1 Samuel 2:9b
[2] Proverbs 3:5,6
[3] Isaiah 50:7

Whereas human strength is limited, God's strength is absolutely unlimited. Moreover, when God's strength is at work, you enjoy a roller-coaster ride. Life becomes so much fun that you don't even get to feel the stress. It is time you soared into the dimension of God's unlimited strength.

At the age of *eighty five*, Caleb initiated an enterprise to dislodge *giants* from their ancestral homes. The younger men may have trusted in their youthful strength. The warriors may have depended on their prowess, skills, and experience. But Caleb's trust rested on God.[1] He understood that with God's help, age would never be a barrier.

The help of God will definitely take you beyond the limits imposed by your natural weaknesses and deficiencies. I therefore encourage you today to learn how to surrender to God and yield to His Strength.

The journey is very far, and the calling is too high; many faint and perish on the way, not because God is unable, but because they trusted in their flesh.[2]

---

[1] Joshua 14:12
[2] Psalm 147:10,11; Isaiah 40:28-31

You cannot gain *spiritual and prophetic wisdom* by your own efforts.

You cannot *pray effectually* by your own strength.

You cannot *believe for miracles* by your own strength.

You cannot walk in *personal holiness* by your own power.

You cannot experience *financial abundance* by your own strength and struggles.

You cannot see *growth and fruitfulness in your life* by mere physical exertion.

"For by strength shall no man prevail..."

When you operate in your natural strength, life is a battle, and a race. On the other hand, when you operate in the strength of the Lord, life is a sweet experience.

Therefore, put your hope, your trust, and your confidence in God. He never grows tired or weary. He neither sleeps nor slumbers, and He will never fail you if you depend upon Him for help.[1]

King David served as an excellent model of this dependence on God when he declared, "I love You, O Lord,

---

[1] Psalm 147:10,11

my strength"[1] He understood that when the God is your strength, the battles and pressures of life easily bow to you.

When the Lord becomes your strength, the seven-fold dimensions of His wisdom become operational in you, and you gain unlimited access to uncommon solutions.

As the Lord becomes your strength, you begin to pray without ceasing, and manifest tremendous miracles on the earth.

As the Lord becomes your strength, your light begins to shine in pure personal holiness, notwithstanding the corruption in the world.

As the Lord becomes your strength, you move from the realm of surviving into that of thriving, in spite of your earthly circumstances.

As the Lord becomes your strength, you begin to bloom and blossom with beautiful and enviable results.

Knowing the demand and challenges of the journey, God gave us an able Helper - the Holy Spirit. His job is to

---

[1] Psalm 18:1

encourage, inspire, strengthen, and enable us to fulfil our destiny in Christ.[1]

The Spirit of the Lord – the Holy Spirit – is the strength of the Lord.

His Spirit is His strength!

Now, the secret to this strength is *surrender*. Surrender is the greatest challenge of the Christian walk. The reason it is so daunting and tough is that we are scared to let go and let God take over; and sadly, what glories, peace, rest, abundance, favours, and blessings we forfeit thereby.

Help us to surrender, Oh Lord!

Now, here are some helpful guidelines on how to surrender:

#1. Spend time in worship.

As you spend time in worship before God, the Holy Spirit broods over your heart and softens it – *it's such an indescribable experience*.

In His presence, the passion to obey God begins to grow. In His presence, the power to obey God begins to grow too.

---

[1] Psalms 46:1; John 14:16; 2 Corinthians 3:17; Hebrews 13:6

#2. Act upon His instructions even when you don't want to and it seems difficult.

Each time you act on God's voice in your heart, against your own will, something in you is broken, and your depth of surrender to Him grows.

#3. Wait upon Him in fasting, prayer, and meditation.

Prolonged periods of fasting and praying, accompanied with worship and meditation on God's words, do something to your spirit, soul, and body, which enables you to surrender to God.

#4. Follow men and women of God of total surrender.

There are spiritual men and women in your midst - who have died to this world and to the flesh. Stay under their leadership. Follow their examples. Listen to them. Learn from them. Imitate them.

Surrender to the Lord is contagious: On the long run, as you interact with people of deep surrender, you catch their spirit and their strength.

#5. Ask the Holy Spirit for help!

Oh, this is absolutely powerful. The Holy Spirit is our Helper. God has given Him to help us in any and every way, just as long as we are willing to reach out to Him for help; so, learn to employ His help.

Stop struggling by yourself, and ask the Holy Spirit to take over and do His job in your life.

How do you do this?

Well, simply say 'Oh Lord help me!'

Yes, it's that simple.

Do you find it difficult to pray? Ask Him for help.

Do you find it hard to read and understand the Bible? Then ask Him to help you.

Do you have problems with a besetting sin? He is there to help.

Do you have problems with growing your business? Invite His assistance.

Do you have problems in your home and relationships? Seek His help.

Are you stagnant and struggling financially? Ask Him to help you out.

Are you having a rough time with your schooling? He can help.

Are you terrified by the uncertainties of tomorrow? He knows exactly how to help you. Get Him involved.

The most powerful prayer I've ever prayed in my life has continued to be *'Lord help me.'*

Asking for His help is an act of humility. Humility is wisdom, and attracts the help of God.

Some may trust in their chariots and horses - physical talents, looks, and connections. That should not bother you. You may not have those; but you have the Helper. Therefore, you are not disadvantaged in any way.

Though the thought '*I can'* may appear to be cool and cute, choose rather to believe that *He can*; because, yes, *He can*.

Let the Holy Spirit of God be your gift and your talent. Let Him be your beauty, and your advantage; and yes, let the Lord Himself be your strength.

11th Key

Pray in the Spirit

One of the fundamental emphases of this book is the importance of praying and fasting as vital keys to unlocking God's uncommon solutions in our lives.

However, ordinary mechanical and religious prayers will not get you very far in life, and neither will praying with your mere senses.

Victorious Christians are those that have moved beyond the mere routine of prayer into the dimension of praying in the Spirit.

So, you must learn to pray in the Spirit.[1]

Now, what exactly is praying in the Spirit?

It is being full of the Holy Spirit and yielding to His guidance and instructions in prayer.

It is praying in the energy and power of the Holy Spirit.

---

[1] Ephesians 6:18; Jude 20

It is listening to the Holy Spirit in prayer and saying exactly what He wants you to say.

It is praying in other tongues during prayers. When you are praying in other tongues, your senses may not be aware of what you are saying; your spirit is uttering mysteries to God.[1]

The Holy Spirit helps our weaknesses - that is, our ignorance of what to pray for. He intercedes for us under such circumstances as He is allowed to take control.[2]

He knows exactly what God wants you to have at each point in time; so, He reveals to you what you should demand in prayer.[3]

Here are some practical guidelines for praying in the Spirit:

#1. Begin with deep, heart-felt, and totally surrendered worship.

Whenever you worship Jesus Christ, you attract and activate the person and power of the Holy Spirit.

Worship is the river in which the Holy Spirit swims.

---

[1] 1 Corinthians 14:2
[2] Romans 8:26
[3] 1 Corinthians 2:11,12

Therefore, learn to spend time in worship before moving into any other form of prayers.

#2. Develop a listening and attentive heart.

Whenever you feel and perceive the presence of the Holy Spirit, you should let Him speak: In pictures, songs, scriptures, prayer points, and prophecies - within your heart. Then flow accordingly.

#3. Learn to yield your tongue to Him.

The Holy Spirit will often bypass your senses to utter mysteries directly to God. At such times, you will find yourself praying and singing in other tongues.

As you go through #1 to #3 again, and again, and again, you will experience His influence growing more powerful and edifying with each new cycle.

In the end, there is great peace and deep assurance of faith that you have received what you have prayed for; and, in addition, you are being built up in your most holy faith.[1]

---

[1] Jude 20

12th Key

Fear God

I absolutely love Psalm 25:12-14; so I will quote it in full below. Note emphases are mine.

"Who, then, are *those who fear the Lord*? He will instruct them in the ways they should choose. *They will spend their days in prosperity*, and their descendants will inherit the land. The Lord confides in those who fear him; he makes his covenant known to them."

Did you notice the connection between the fear of God and endless prosperity? In other words, if you want to spend your days in prosperity, it begins with the fear of God.

I would describe the fear of God here primarily in terms of our attitude towards His person, His words, and those things that are associated with Him.

The fear of God is rooted in a humble heart, and manifests in obedience to the word of the Lord.

Unfortunately, many who claim to be Christians today lack the fear of God.

For instance, speaking in terms of God's words, how can someone have the fear of God and yet wilfully and continuously persist in wrongdoing?[1] How can someone have the fear of God and neglect the gathering of believers?[2] How can someone have the fear of God and dishonour men and women of God?[3] How can someone have the fear of God and steal their tithes?

No wonder many who claim to be Christians today live such weak and defeated lives. Yes, because the fear of God is the foundation for enduring success, wealth, and prosperity.

Those who claim to be Christians, but lack the fear of God, live in lack and defeat because they are functioning like everyone else.

Look at Psalm 25:12-14 again:

---

[1] 2 Timothy 2:19
[2] Hebrews 10:25
[3] Hebrews 13:17

"Who, then, are *those who fear the Lord*? He will instruct them in the ways they should choose. *They will spend their days in prosperity*, and their descendants will inherit the land. The Lord confides in those who fear him; he makes his covenant known to them."

So, the fear of the Lord releases the instructions of God.

I've observed that it is very difficult to receive divine guidance when you lack the fear of God.

The reason a lot of God's children do not hear the voice of God, and do not know His will for their lives, is that they lack the fear of God.

The fear of God is your access to His instructions. This means that those who do not fear God have no access to His guidance. So, they have no access to His uncommon solutions that make life a bed of roses.

You see, when the fear of God is in your heart, He begins to instruct you in the way chosen for you. Then you begin to spend your days in prosperity as a result of walking in the ways of the Lord revealed to you.[1]

Now, look at that fourteenth verse:

"The Lord *confides* in those who fear him; he makes his covenant known to them."

It clearly reveals the depth of intimacy with God enjoyed by those who fear Him. That is to say that the fear of the Lord is the key to intimacy with God.[2]

The Holy Spirit will draw near to, and ultimately become intimate with an individual that fears God. Then His wisdom begins to flow into and through you as He confides in you and makes His covenant known to you.

Wisdom, undoubtedly, is the principal thing for success and leads to phenomenal wealth. However, the fear of the Lord is the beginning of wisdom![3]

So, if the fear of God is not in you, His wisdom will elude you. This is because He can only confide in those who fear

---

[1] Psalm 25:12,13,14
[2] Psalm 25:14
[3] Psalm 111:10; Proverbs 9:10

Him.[1] When you fear God, He will reveal His secrets to you, and this will distinguish you.

As you can see, there's a direct path from the fear of God, to wisdom, and then to wealth.

---

[1] Psalm 25:14

13th Key

Clean Up!

Once upon a time, God sent a prophet named Jonah to prophesy against a city called Nineveh. This city was so sinful that the prophet expected it to be destroyed in spite of his warnings. Surprisingly, the Ninevites believed God, declared a fast, and all of them, from the greatest to the least put on sackcloth and sat down in the dust as a mark of their repentance.[1]

When God saw what they did and how they turned from their evil ways, He had compassion and did not bring upon them the destruction He had threatened.[2]

I would like you to observe that what moved God was not just that they fasted, but also the fact that they turned from their evil ways.

Fasting and praying are powerful keys to uncommon solutions, but your fasting and praying would be

---

[1] Jonah 3:5-10
[2] Johan 3:10

acceptable to God only if you turn from those things that are against His ways.

If we want to see the Lord's compassion, and gain access to His uncommon solutions, it is not just enough to fast and pray; we must equally turn from our evil ways.

In fact, one of the most important things you must do during any fast, particularly lengthy ones, is to review your life in the light of the commandments of God.[1]

A season of fasting is a time for soul-searching, repentance, and contrition; a time for thorough spiritual and moral cleansing.

Relationships that are opposed to His ways and commandments must be forsaken.

Behaviours that contravene His laws must be repented of and rejected.

Every weight that hinder your peace with God must be thrown off; every besetting sin must be put off.[2]

___

[1] Psalms 139:23-24
[2] Hebrews 12:1

Stop meddling with unclean things. Stop defiling yourself. Stop sinning against God.

Speak the truth from your heart and deceive no more. Put all lies and falsehood away from your life.[1]

Turn from impurities, every immorality and lust. Repentance is the surest and fastest key to restoration; but it must be sincere, and total.

If you want to enjoy a continuous flow of God's uncommon solutions and supernatural interventions in your life, you would have to clean up your *heart*, your *mind*, and your *actions*.

Our God is gracious and compassionate.[2] He is slow to anger and abounding in love. If you return in sincere humility and contrition, He will relent from sending calamity.

Practical holiness and moral purity should be a major goal of every fasting season of yours.

---

[1] Psalm 15;2
[2] Exodus 34:6; 2 Chronicles 30:9; Nehemiah 9:17; Psalm 86:15; 103:8; 111:4; 145:8; Joel 2:13; Jonah 4:2

Make every effort to live in peace with all men and to be holy; without holiness no one will see the Lord.[1]

Let me repeat that last line: *without holiness no one will see the Lord.*

To see God means to enjoy fellowship with Him, as well as to experience His power and glory. Holiness, therefore, is a major condition for intimacy with God - and hence, for supernatural manifestations.

Holiness was the major reason for the level of intimacy that Jesus enjoyed with His Father and the level of supernatural manifestations He commanded while on earth.

His life on earth was a testimony of stainless spiritual and moral purity.[2] That was why He enjoyed an unparalleled height of supernatural glory during His earthly ministry.

You and I have been called to walk with God here on earth as Jesus did; as He is so are we in this world.[1] For that reason, we must make every effort to be holy.

---

[1] Hebrews 12:14
[2] John 8:46; Hebrews 4:15

Nevertheless the foundation of God standeth sure, having this seal, The Lord knoweth them that are his. And, Let everyone that nameth the name of Christ depart from iniquity.[2]

As Christians, and particularly with regards to praying and fasting, it is our personal responsibility to proactively and responsively move away from any possibility of spiritual and moral defilement.

You and I cannot afford to be calling on the name of the Lord, and still be toying with sin; the consequences are just too grave and devastating.

In a large house there are articles not only of gold and silver, but also of wood and clay; some are for noble purposes and some for ignoble. *If a man cleanses himself from the latter, he will be an instrument for noble purposes, made holy, useful to the Master and prepared to do any good work.*[3]

If a man cleanses himself…

---

[1] 1 John 4:17
[2] 2 Timothy 2:19
[3] 2 Timothy 2:20-21

So, the issue of spiritual and moral purity is not something you can afford to leave to chance. It is not a matter for wishing either. *It is your duty to cleanse yourself.* That is one of the major reasons God introduced the mystery of fasting and 'sackcloth'.

A time of fasting should include quality sessions devoted to humble contrition for confession of, and repentance from known and unknown sins.

Spiritual and moral purity should be a major goal of every fasting season of yours.

Imagine the grace that could be yours if only you would stop clinging to worthless idols and holding on to empty distractions.[1]

How far have your idols brought you - those things you lean on? Isn't it time you returned to the Lord? Are you not yet tired of your backslidings and frustrations? Aren't you yet weary of your sins and hypocrisies?

Return and He will have mercy upon you. Call upon Him and He will answer you. Repent and He will restore you.

---

[1] Jonah 2:8

14th Key

Shun Worldliness

Demas was a friend of Apostle Paul, as well as his fellow worker.[1] Like Timothy, Titus, and Luke, he was a very close companion of Paul; so he must have heard some of the greatest revelations of the New Testament, and witnessed some of the most amazing miracles from one of the greatest Apostles of all time.

We would therefore expect this man to be one of the staunchest, most faithful, and fruitful Christians of the New Testament - like Timothy, Titus, Mark, and Luke.

Alas, this was not the case; he was lured away by worldliness.[2] Worldliness destroyed his very colorful destiny. He deserted Apostle Paul, and turned his back on God because of the things of this world.

You must be on your guard against worldliness. It is a killer and a destroyer of destinies.

What is worldliness?

---

[1] Colossians 4:14; Philemon 1:23,24
[2] 2 Timothy 4:10

#1: Worldliness is your loving the world and the things in the world.[1]

Genesis 34 contains a clear illustration of what happens to those who love the world. It tells of Dinah, Jacob's only daughter who strayed from the safety of her home because of her thirst for the things of this world. In the end, she got raped by an uncircumcised man. It is a very sad story lust, vengeance, and destruction.

What are you looking for in the world?

The world is empty, dry, and tasteless. It has nothing of eternal value to offer you.

The psalmist understood this when he said, "Whom have I in heaven but you? And earth has nothing I desire besides you."[2]

Set your mind, rather, on things above, not on earthly things.[3]

---

[1] 1 John 2: 15-17
[2] Psalm 73:25
[3] Colossians 3:2

#2: Worldliness is your having the same values and priorities as the world.[1]

That means you make your choices and decisions - for instance, regarding career, location, job, or marriage - based primarily on what is highly valued among men.

This kind of individual is detestable in the sight of God.

#3: Worldliness is your pursuing other things at the expense of the Kingdom of God.[2]

Every Christian who places earthly concerns above Kingdom interests is worldly, and will ultimately desert God unless such worldliness is checked.

You must daily seek God's purifying grace in your life. Pray to Him daily to purify your heart and strengthen you against the seductions of this world.[3]

What you feed your mind also matters.

The books you read, the music you listen to, the people and things you interact with, either fuel spirituality in your life, or feed worldliness.

---

[1] Luke 16:15
[2] Matthew 6:33
[3] Psalm 51:10

Another great antidote to worldliness is daily meditation on God's words .[1] So also is intimate fellowship with Him through worship.

Through years of studying God's words and observing people, both in life and ministry, I have learnt that people who place God's values and interests above those of this world, enjoy unbridled access to His uncommon solutions.

If you will shun worldliness and honour God by not going your own way, and not doing as you please or speaking idle words, you will find your joy in the Lord. Then He will cause you to ride on the heights of the land, and to feast on the inheritance of your father Jacob.[2]

---

[1] Romans 12:2
[2] Isaiah 58:13,14

15th Key

Humbly Accept God's Word

On a certain day of the fifty four days of fasting and praying that I referred to at the beginning of this book, as I was interceding for different people, I saw a vision of a human brain wrapped up in a very dense black cloud.

In the vision, I was told that the cloud was hindering the entrance of God's words into the mind of some of the people I was interceding for.

As I watched and listened, wondering at what the dense dark cloud meant, I heard the Lord say, "This is *dark knowledge*, known in human language as *pride*."

He then opened my mind to understand the mysteries of pride, good understanding, submission, and divine favour.

What we call pride is actually a form of knowledge - that is, the essence of pride is knowledge. Knowledge, whether accurate or not, is the substance that pride is made of. However, it is a form of knowledge that is spiritually darkened.

The *darkness* of this knowledge is not a matter of accuracy, but that of whether or not it allows you to recognize and embrace God's word when it is revealed.

When what you know prevents you from accepting and obeying God's words, then that knowledge has become pride.

Knowledge puffs up.[1]

When it is left unbridled and allowed to puff up, knowledge morphs into pride and becomes a lethal spiritual poison - that is, *the dense dark cloud I saw in the vision.* At this point it begins to attract divine opposition and humiliation.

Pride goes before destruction, a haughty spirit before a fall.[2]

Pride is a dangerous poison to our relationship with God, with others, with ourselves, and with our environment.

Nevertheless, the most destructive danger of pride is how it poisons our relationship with God, and impedes our metamorphosis.

---

[1] 1 Corinthians 8:1
[2] Proverbs 16:18

On the one hand pride attracts the hostility and opposition of God; on the other hand it hinders metamorphosis.

When *any* knowledge mutates and darkens into pride in the mind, it exalts itself against the knowledge and revelation of God. Then, God is compelled to knock it down.

God hates pride![1]

A clear example of the operation of pride, and its destructive nature with respect to our relationship with God, is seen in the story of Cain and Abel. Both of them had a relationship with God, and both were *worshippers*. Abel, however, had *faith* in his heart, while Cain had *pride*.

The bible tells us that 'by faith Abel offered God a better sacrifice than Cain did.'[2] The same bible also tells us that 'faith comes by hearing the word of God.'[3] So, it is safe to conclude that the brothers had received God's word regarding what to offer. Abel humbly believed and accepted the word of God. Cain did not.

Not only did God ask them to bring an offering, *He let them know exactly what He wanted them to bring.*

---

[1] 1 Peter 5:5; Leviticus 26:19-20
[2] Hebrews 11:4
[3] Romans 10:17

Abel believed and obeyed.

Cain, on the other hand, insisted on doing it His own way. His own way was that of giving God *what he had*, rather than giving God what *God required*.

Most Christians today are still trapped in this error. Entrenched pseudo piousness teaches us to give God *what we have*. Divine revelation on the other hand teaches us to offer God *what He wants*.

...and find out what pleases the Lord.[1]

Cain gave to God. He sacrificed an offering to the Lord, but failed to obtain God's favour, because he didn't give God what He had asked for. More so, when God offered him the opportunity to correct himself, he refused to accept God's ways.[2]

Many Christians today are *giving to God*, and *serving Him sacrificially*, but still fail to attract His favours. This is because, like Cain, they insist on offering Him *what they have*, instead of *what He wants*.

Cain is an example of men and women that insist on serving God on their own terms. Their hearts and minds

---

[1] Ephesians 5:10
[2] Genesis 4:6-7

are stubborn and hardened by pride. Such people never grow spiritually. Their lives are stagnant. They remain on the same spot from year to year.

Wherever you see stagnation, you are most likely looking at a proud person.

Check your life. If you notice any areas of serious stagnation, then there is *something that you know* that is stopping *certain divine knowledge* from entering your heart. In other words, pride is hiding there somewhere!

And pride is destructive.

Pride goes before destruction, a haughty spirit before a fall.[1]

However, you don't have to be destroyed. You can live a humble life that is free from the poison of pride.

Here's how: Allow the word of God to enter your mind, to fill your heart, and to shape your thoughts and actions.

Let the word of Christ dwell in you richly[2]

This is the way to grow spiritually and enjoy continuous divine evolution.

---

[1] Proverbs 16:18
[2] Colossians 3:16

It means to humbly accept the Word.[1]

The process is simple: exalt the word in your mind. Don't argue it; just submit to it.

Accept it as it is.

This humble acceptance of the authority of God's word defeats pride and unlocks the fountains of *good understanding.* This in turn releases the favour of God and His uncommon solutions in your life; since, according to the scriptures, "good understanding giveth favour: but the way of transgressors is hard."[2]

Good understanding is the opposite of the *dark knowledge* called pride. It is the understanding that comes from faith and the humble acceptance of God's word in our hearts.

By faith we understand...[3]

When it comes to God's word, faith must precede understanding. To do otherwise would amount to pride, perpetual spiritual blindness, and stagnation in life.

Accept and believe first, unquestioningly. Submit all contrary, thoughts, opinions, and perspectives to the

---

[1] James 1:21
[2] Proverbs 13:15
[3] Hebrews 11:3

superiority of God's revelations. Then watch as the Light of God's knowledge and good understanding flood your soul with uncommon solutions!

16th Key

Seek God's Ways

Prophecies create *expectations* that can either get fulfilled or not; and both possibilities are clearly shown in the Scriptures.

Obviously, the first possibility - *For surely there is an end; and thine expectation shall not be cut off*[1] – would bring joy, happiness, and exultation.

The other possibility - *You expected much, but see, it turned out to be little*[2] – on the other hand, of course, would lead to frustration, disillusionment, and sadness.

Over the years, with respect to prophecies and their manifestations, I've had people ask me, "Why didn't so and so prophecies come to pass in my life?"

Well, here are some lights on how genuine prophecies from God work.

---

[1] Proverbs 23:18
[2] Haggai 1:9

A prophecy is a preview of the destination of a certain way. It is a description of the features and ultimate end of a path.

Every road leads to somewhere and has several landmarks along it. Where a road leads to is called its destination - from where we get the word destiny.

You cannot separate a road from its destination, as both are inextricably linked.

Consequently, when someone begins to walk along a certain road, you can - if you know that way - correctly predict his experiences, as well his destination- if he continues along that way.

Moreso, your prediction will be right, not because people have ends, but because roads, ways, and pathways do!

People have free wills, and can move away from any way, thereby disconnecting from the destination of such a way.

Hence, it is ways, not people, which are predestined. Roads, ways, and paths are predestined; people are not.

God knows the end from the beginning of every road; thus, He can reveal these destinations.[1] These revelations then become what men receive as prophecies.

---

[1] Isaiah 46:10

Prophecies, therefore, are previews of the destinations of ways. They are descriptions of the features and ultimate ends of paths.

Prophecy is a divine way of saying, "If you keep travelling along so and so road, you will meet this and that, experience so and so, and reach here and there."

For instance: "*In the way* of righteousness there is life; *along that path* is immortality."[1]

You need to understand that it is paths and ways that are pre-destined, not people.

When God wants you to experience certain blessings, He *calls* you to *walk along certain ways*.[2] God prepares His destinations, and designs *His ways* to them. Then He calls you by His words and instructions[3] to walk on *His ways*.

The moment you get on that way, you become a partaker of the blessings and destinations of the way.

It is the pictures of these blessings and destinations that we receive through the Spirit as prophecies.

---

[1] Proverbs 12:28
[2] Isaiah 30:21
[3] Romans 8:29, 30

So, it is not enough to celebrate prophecies. We must, like the wise, *ask for His ways*.

Ordinary folks get excited and carried away by the power and beauty of prophetic declarations. Wise and extraordinary people on the other hand move beyond that to seek His ways.

The wise thank God for the prophecies, but still ask, "Lord, what must I do to realize this in my life?"

Moses earnestly sought God's ways.[1] No wonder he commanded such uncommon solutions and extraordinary manifestations on the earth. He understood that God reveals Himself through His ways, that is, His words.

God's ways constitute what is referred to in the previous chapter as *good understanding*, which is what releases His favours.[2]

You cannot enjoy His favours except you are walking in His ways.

Like David, we must seek His ways.[3]

---

[1] Exodus 33:13
[2] Proverbs 13:15
[3] Psalms 86:11

God's ends are inextricably linked to His ways. When we forsake His ways, we forfeit His ends.

We must, therefore, actively seek, find, and walk in His ways.[1]

On the day of Pentecost, Peter delivered a very lengthy and powerful sermon filled with promises and prophecies. He previewed beautiful and mouth-watering ends and destinations of God.[2]

In the process, however, he forgot to point out the way to those destinations!

Nonetheless, his listeners had enough mental sophistication to ask for the way - "What shall we do to be saved?"[3]

This is what it means to seek His ways. I call that wisdom.

The Philippian Jailer also demonstrated similar good spiritual sense when he asked, "Sirs, what must I do to be saved?"

---

[1] Jeremiah 6:16
[2] Acts 2:1-36
[3] Acts 2:37

Would you command uncommon solutions and extraordinary manifestations on the earth? Then, get committed to seeking, finding, and walking in God's ways.

17th Key

Be Merciful

You and I are objects of God's mercies through the love of Jesus Christ, and by our faith in Him.[1]

However, it is not just enough to rejoice about this; it also confers on us a serious responsibility to become dispensers of the same mercies.

God makes us objects of His mercies, so that we can become His channels of mercy and compassion to others.

If you have received God's mercies, compassion, and forgiveness, you must show gratitude to Him by extending the same to others.

Be merciful: Intercede for other people before God, and others. Forgive those who have wronged you. Be more patient and tolerant with other people's flaws and faults.

The bible is full of challenges to us to be merciful.[2]

---

[1] Romans 9:22-24
[2] Matthew 5:7; Matthew 6:12-15; Mathew 18:21-35; Luke 13:6-9; James 2:13

Mercy, really, is all about making room for change and God's work in other people's lives.[1]

The more merciful we are towards the weak, the more we receive God's wisdom to become agents of transformation.

"We who are strong ought to bear with the failings of the weak and not to please ourselves."[2]

Sometimes, the weak and slow among us are there to develop and test our patience!

Joshua and Caleb would have made it to the Promised Land in three days, but because of the doubts of their brethren, they spent forty years on the way. That is the price of love and relationship.

There were over two million people walking through the Red Sea - including pregnant mothers, children, goats, and livestock. They were in no position to run!

Sometimes, we are slowed down by others; but that is what mercy is all about.

Relationships can be quite expensive. The weaknesses of those you love will often slow you down one way or the

---

[1] Luke 13:6-9
[2] Romans 15:1

other; you must be prepared for that. It is the cost of love, mercy, and compassion.

Mercy enables us to think and care about others. It is necessary if we want to help others into the Promised Land, even if we could have gotten there faster. It is all about love, compassion, and tolerance.

Sometimes, we need to give up our privileges so that others can make it.

We need to share the word and the vision of God with others. Furthermore, we may need to constantly prod them to put their trust in God until success is achieved.

That is the ministry of mercy.

It takes courage and boldness to be merciful. Often, it is fear and insecurity that make us intolerant and judgemental of other people. We are afraid we would not be able to handle their faults and the attendant consequences.

So we turn into moral tyrants!

In order to be merciful, we must have a bold vision of the potentials and possibilities of others – this is the lesson in the parable of the barren tree.[1]

---

[1] Luke 13:6-9

Jesus did not condemn the woman that was caught in adultery.[1] Instead, He dealt with her in a manner that teaches us to see things in others - and in ourselves - that are not yet obvious.

To create a beautiful world, we must believe in God; but we must also believe in ourselves and in other people's capacities to become better and greater.

When coupled with our sense of gratitude for the love of Jesus Christ, this bold vision of possibilities in others will empower us to be very merciful.

This heart of mercy in turn will release more mercies from God upon us, resulting in diverse miracles and uncommon solutions, for, *"Blessed are the merciful, for they will be shown mercy."*[2]

---

[1] John 8:1-11
[2] Matthew 5:7

18th Key

Mind Your Own Business

Sometime ago, I noticed lots of young adults within the Christian community that were still depending on their parents for a hundred percent of their financial sustenance.

At the time, I thought it was such a shameful and disgraceful state of affairs. I still think that it is a totally unacceptable and inexcusable condition of things.

It is totally unacceptable for a young adult of twenty one and above to depend on anybody other than God and himself or herself for financial sustenance.

How can someone who ought to have become a parent by now still be depending on parents for sustenance?

A lot of Christians are too lazy and unproductive for God's liking. I observed this trend particularly among the praying and fasting lot who have the tendency to mask their laziness, idleness, and lack of productivity behind a facade of praying and fasting. This does not glorify God in any way.

Thanks to my parents; I have been praying and fasting since I was three. This book was written during a season of praying and fasting that lasted for fifty four days. As a matter of fact, as you might have observed in the pages of this book, *I am a staunch advocate of the power of praying and fasting to create uncommon solutions.*

However, it is quite disgraceful to see otherwise smart and productive people morph into brainless religious drones all in the name of praying and fasting.

The kind of praying and fasting that pleases God is the kind that results in productivity and profitability.

According to the bible, land that drinks in the rain often falling on it and that produces a crop useful to those for whom it is farmed receives the blessing of God. But land that produces thorns and thistles is worthless and is in danger of being cursed. In the end it will be burned.[1]

The rain here represents all of the various blessings you have received in the Lord, such as, teachings, prophecies, prayers, laying on of hands, salvation, the Holy Spirit, spiritual gifts, and so on.

So, what have you produced out of God's deposits and investments in your life?

---

[1] Hebrews 6:7-8

What has God's presence in your life amounted to?

What are the uncommon and supernatural outcomes of your praying and fasting?

Where is the wisdom of God in you?

Where are your skills?

Where is your courage?

Where is your faith?

Don't be idle and lazy so as not to attract a curse to yourself!

I'm certain that by now, if you are a bible-believing, praying and fasting Christian, after all you've seen and heard from the Lord, you *ought to have* become the chief sponsor of your family.

The anointing of the Holy Spirit upon your life is not just for speaking in tongues and emotional vibrations; it is also the power to *create wealth*[1].

It is not just the power to heal, or cast out devils; it is also the power to slay the giants of lack and produce abundance.

---

[1] Deuteronomy 8:18

Our God is increase-oriented, multiplication-oriented, profit-oriented, and success-oriented.

When done properly, in humility, wisdom, and faith, the rewards of praying and fasting are absolutely inestimable.

Genuine praying and fasting should result in an increased level of energy, drive, motivation, speed, and enthusiasm to pursue God's dreams for your life and achieve greatness to His glory.[1]

Also, when done in the right spirit and attitude, praying and fasting should result in life-transforming revelations, divine instructions, and ideas that will turn your life into a wonder on earth.

So, it is very important during a time of fasting, to seek God's wisdom regarding *what to do*.

I say this because God can only bless the *work of your hands;*[2] but don't just fold your hands waiting for God to show you what to do.

Be proactive. Look around you. What can you do? What is in your hand?

---

[1] Isaiah 40:31
[2] Deuteronomy 28:12; Psalm 1:3

"Whatever your hand finds to do, do it with all your might..."[1]

Find something and give it your best shot; stick to it. Be diligent in it that your profiting may appear.[2]

Trust and believe God to teach you how to profit in life, in business, in ministry, and in your personal finances.[3]

Even the spiritual gifts are given for profit and not just for religious ceremonies, rituals, and entertainment. The spiritual gifts of God in you should produce spiritual and material profits.

"...but the manifestation of the Spirit is given to every man *to profit* withal."[4]

Now pray:

"Lord, teach my hands to create wealth and to profit."

.2.

---

[1] Eccl. 9:10
[2] 1 Timothy 4:15
[3] Isaiah 48:17
[4] 1 Corinthians 12:7

The importance of the *work of your hands* with respect to God's blessings and prosperity in your life can never be overstated.

The 'work of your hands', that is, 'whatever you do', would include the goods, products, and services that you create through your ingenuity, hard work, efforts, thinking, and other kindred activities; but it also includes your *plans*.

In other words, the *plans* that you create in order to realize God's dreams for your life, can accurately be called the works of your hands.

The following scripture from proverbs shows that it is your responsibility to plan.

"To man belong the plans of the heart, but from the Lord comes the reply of the tongue."[1]

It is one thing to have a dream, or a goal; however, it is another thing to have a concrete plan to accomplish that dream.

---

[1] Proverbs 16:1

Put in another way, it is one thing to have, say, *a sound business idea*, it is quite another matter to have *a sound business plan* to turn that idea into profit.

Many Christians have good ideas but lack an adequate plan to turn their ideas into *profitable enterprises*.

You see, even if you have the best of ideas, God's blessings will only rest on those ideas if you have a sound plan to convert them into profit.

David had the desire and vision to build a temple for the Lord. But he also put a plan in place to translate his dream into a reality!

King David rose to his feet and said: "Listen to me, my brothers and my people. I had it in my heart to build a house as a place of rest for the ark of the covenant of the Lord, for the footstool of our God, and I made plans to build it."[1]

I'd like you to notice that David didn't just have the dream in his heart to build a house for God; he also *made plans* for the project.

---

[1] 1 Chronicles 28:2

The Spirit of God inspired the ideas for building the temple in David's heart. David then engaged his mental faculties to make the plans for building that temple.

When God inspires an idea in your heart, it is your responsibility to make plans to achieve that idea.

As I have already pointed out, the plans that you make are aspects of *the work of your hands*; and God is committed to blessing them.[1]

Praying and fasting are powerful spiritual tools for productivity and profiting. However, they will never take the place of meticulous and accurate planning.

As a matter of fact, praying and fasting, when done properly, actually enhance and empower planning.

Many that are fasting and praying, are failing to plan as well. The result is that while their praying and fasting invoke powerful spiritual forces in their behalf, these forces lack the channels to release the material benefits of their praying and fasting.

---

[1] Psalms 20:4

The main reason many fail to plan is because *planning is a very tedious and mentally exhausting task.* Planning demands a vigorous exercise of the mind – something only very few individuals are willing to undertake, particularly within religious circles!

Ideas that freely drop into your mind from God may require little or no effort on your part. However, when it comes to the issue of planning, you must sit down and tenaciously articulate information, ideas, facts, data, counsels, and so on, to develop a practical and workable plan to turn your ideas to profit.

.3.

Here's what the Apostle Paul wrote to the Thessalonians Church:

"For even when we were with you, we gave you this rule: *'if a man will not work, he shall not eat.* We hear that some among you are idle. They are not busy; they are busybodies. Such people we command and urge in the Lord Jesus Christ to *settle down and earn the bread they eat.*"[1]

---

[1] 2 Thessalonians 3:10-12

Yes, settle down and *earn the bread you eat*. The rule is that the one who does not work should not eat.

Note that it is a rule.[1]

You have no right to food if you *can* work but aren't productively and profitably occupied.

Stop looking for free food and handouts. That is pathetic and ungodly.

Praying and fasting is not an exemption from productivity and profitability. In fact, I believe that those who pray and fast regularly should be more productive than others, since, after all, they are supposed to have deeper access to divine mysteries and wisdom.

So, settle down and become productive.

Now, it is impossible to become productive without a product. That ought to be obvious when you consider the fact that productivity comes from the word *product*.

So, without products, there can be no productivity; no productivity, no wealth; no products, no wealth.

Those who lack products will always lack sufficient cash.

---

[1] 2 Thessalonians 3:10

Products are the offspring of the combinations of your talents, skills, knowledge, abilities, and experiences. They are what you create out of those combinations in order to solve specific human problems.

The scriptural productivity phrase *'whatever your hand finds to do'*[1], refers to what you can do, plus the problems you can solve with what you can do.

The word 'finds' suggests that what you are looking for is hidden. In other words, what you can do might not be as obvious as you may think.

Also, the problems you can solve with what you can do are not obvious.

You may have to search for these things; in fact, you may have to ask God to open your eyes to see what you can do.

A time of praying and fasting, therefore, should not just be used to pray for your needs to be met, rather it should incorporate the *searching* for, and *finding* of answers.

You need answers to such vital questions as:

What can I do? That is to say, what are my *abilities*?

---

[1] Ecclesiastes 9:10

Then, what can I do with what I can do? In other words, what *problems* can be solved using my abilities?

So, what *problems* can your *abilities* solve?

Human beings have problems.

Families have problems.

Institutions have problems.

Small businesses have problems.

Big businesses have problems.

Nations have problems.

Which of these problems can be solved by the various combinations of your talents, skills, knowledge, abilities, and experiences?

If you are certain that you can solve those problems, then approach those concerned with an offer.

Yes, it is that simple.

Put a reasonable price-tag on your products, solutions, offers, services, or whatever they are. Ensure, however, that this price-tag allows you to make a profit.

Now, don't settle there. Continue to focus on improving your solutions in all of their strategic aspects. This is the essence of productivity and profitability.[1]

Also, think of how you can improve the quality and effectiveness of your solutions as well as how you can increase the speed with which you deliver your solutions.

You should also think of how you can increase the number of people enjoying and paying for your solutions.

Don't forget to think of how to lower the price of your products while at the same time increasing your profit margin.

Working is a gift from our Maker that allows us to partner with Him in blessing His creations.

---

[1] 1 Thessalonians 4:11

19th Key

Go For Prophetic Plans

As I've already pointed out, in order to realize the full measure of God's productivity and profiting from your praying and fasting, it is vital that you sit down and develop intelligent and practical plans to turn the ideas of your spirit into profitable enterprises.

Let me now wrap this book up by introducing you to a dimension of plans and planning that should constitute a fasting and praying saint's advantage in the marketplace.

A plan is an organized sequence of actions to be undertaken in order to create an envisaged result. A wise plan is based on accurate facts, plus a pragmatic assessment of practical realities.

One of the most powerful advantages that a Spirit-led, praying and fasting Christian has is access to God's 'ready-made' plans, or what I call *prophetic plans*.

"For I know the plans I have for you", declares the Lord, "plans to prosper you and not to harm you, plans to give you hope and a future."[1].

Clearly, God has His plans for His Children. He has His visions for us, as well as the specific strategies for the realization of those visions and goals.

I'd like you to think of it this way: God has multiple sets of divinely crafted plans for every vision and dream He has put into your heart.

His plans for fulfilling His dreams and visions in your life are by far superior to anything you can conceive in your own natural mind.

"As the heavens are higher than the earth, so are my ways higher than your ways and my thoughts than your thoughts."[2]

Just imagine what it would be like to have ready-made God-crafted plans for each of your dreams and visions.

The exciting truth is that these *God-plans* not only exist, but are also available for you!

---

[1] Jeremiah 29:11
[2] Isaiah 55:9

The spiritual disciplines of fasting, solitude, meditation, and praying, are powerful keys for accessing the Holy Spirit's revelation of these God-plans.

God's own plans are usually prophetic and spiritual; so they don't make much sense to the natural human intellect. Nevertheless, they are infinitely superior to any that the human mind can come up with.

It is these prophetic plans that I have continuously referred to in this book as *uncommon solutions.*

Joshua, the successor to Moses, was an accomplished military general, but he was also a prayer and prophetic warrior who knew the power of a divine plan.

So when confronted by the daunting task of conquering the fortified city of Jericho, he took time out to seek God for His divine victory plans and strategies.[1]

The *God-plans* he obtained must have looked ridiculous to his enemies - and probably to some among his own soldiers.[2] Yet they brought the walls of Jericho down so swiftly their foes didn't know what hit them!

---

[1] Joshua 5:13-15
[2] Joshua 6:1-5

Most times, God's plans seem ridiculous to mere human intellect, but they are exceedingly powerful.

The Holy Spirit is God's agency for revealing His mysterious plans and *uncommon solutions* to His Children.[1] This is why it is important that you build a strong and intimate relationship with the person of the Holy Spirit.

What I'm trying to say is that there are two dimensions of planning:

First, the lower dimension: Here you create and develop your own plans using your mental faculties and capabilities.

Then, the higher dimension: Here you behold God's plans through the revelation of the Holy Spirit, and then download and install them into your mind.

Both dimensions of planning are very powerful and critical to productivity and profitability.

However, the higher dimension of planning is by far superior to the first.

Whereas the individual operating out of the lower dimension of planning is able to walk and run, the one

---

[1] 1 Corinthians 2:9-11

functioning from the higher dimension is able to soar on wings like the eagle!

The difference is clear.

Therefore, in order for your productivity and profitability to manifest at the speed of divinity, learn to employ the higher dimension of planning. Go for prophetic plans.

During your sessions of solitude, fasting, meditations, and prayers, heed the following divine invitation:

"This is what the Lord says, he who made the earth, the Lord who formed it and established it- the Lord is his name: *'Call to me and I will answer you and tell you great and unsearchable things you do not know.'*"[1]

---

[1] Jeremiah 33:2-3

Index

a bold vision, 104
a haughty spirit, 90, 93
A strong faith, 27
Abel, 91, 92
abilities, 116, 117
abundance, 15, 37, 42, 44, 60, 65, 67, 108
accurate facts, 119
actions, 61, 93, 119
agents of change and transformation, 103
Almighty God, 23, 28, 33
angelic visitations, 34
angels, 34
anointed, 14, 17, 60, 61, 62
anointing, 15, 57, 60, 61, 62, 108
answers, 35, 36, 116

barren, 57, 104
be merciful, 102, 104
believe, 65, 94, 105, 110, 115
besetting sin, 69, 80
Besetting sins, 30
bible, 17, 20, 26, 28, 32, 33, 52, 91, 102, 107, 108
Bible, 69
bible meditations, 20
Bible study, 26
Bible study and meditation, 26
Big businesses, 117

blessings, 24, 42, 67, 98, 107, 111, 112
blood, 30
boldness, 104
bread, 114, 115
breath of God, 38
business, 30, 69, 110, 112
busy, 46, 51, 52, 114
busybodies, 114

Cain, 91, 92
Cain and Abel, 91
Caleb, 64, 103
Cana, 12
cares and burdens, 46, 47
choices and decisions, 87
Christ, 17, 19, 24, 67, 83
Christians, 28, 71, 75, 83, 85, 92, 106, 112
compassion, 79, 80, 102, 104
compassionate, 81
confidence, 65
corruption, 66
counsel, 50
courage, 104, 108
create, 13, 108, 110, 111, 116, 119

Daily meditation, 88
Daniel, 33, 34, 35
dark knowledge, 89, 94

darkness, 35, 90
David, 65, 99, 112, 113
Demas, 85
demon spirits, 30
Demonic, 30
demonic forces, 39
demons, 30
destination, 97
destinations, 97, 98, 100
destiny, 29, 32, 34, 63, 67, 85, 97
discover yourself, 52
distractions, 45, 46, 47, 50, 52, 84
divine evolution, 93
divine favour, 89
divine favours, 39, 42
divine guidance, 76
divine idea, 13
divine ideas, 13
divine instructions, 18
divine opposition, 90
divine plan, 121
divine revelation, 32, 34
Divine revelation, 92
divine revelations, 34
doubts, 41
dream, 111, 112, 120
dreams, 11, 30, 109, 111
dreams and visions, 120

earn, 114, 115
earthly things, 86
Egyptians, 10

enemies, 10, 29, 37, 38, 121
enterprise, 64
enterprises, 112, 119
Esther, 28, 29
eternal value, 86
expectations, 59, 96
experience, 15, 42, 65, 82, 98
experiences, 28, 97, 116, 117
extraordinary manifestations, 39, 99, 101, *See* uncommon solutions

faith, 11, 18, 24, 25, 26, 43, 57, 73, 91, 94, 102, 108, 109
Faith, 18, 23, 41, 91
false friends, 39
Families, 117
famine, 24
fast, 28, 33, 79, 80, 89
fasting, 11, 17, 20, 28, 29, 30, 32, 33, 35, 36, 53, 68, 79, 80, 81, 83, 84, 106, 107, 108, 109, 113, 116, 119, 121, 123
Fasting, 26
fasting and praying, 89
favour, 23, 24, 25, 28, 29, 30, 38, 39, 52, 55, 59, 94, 113
Favour, 38
favour in the desert, 23, 27
favours, 55, 67, 92, 99
fear, 39, 74, 75, 76, 77, 78, 104
fears, 41, 77
fellowship with God, 46

finances, 30, 60, 110
financial, 65, 106
financial sustenance, 106
finding answers, 116
focus, 15, 24, 26, 45, 46, 48, 50, 118
food, 58, 59, 115
forces of darkness
spiritual wickedness, 50
forgiveness, 102
forgiving others, 102
fortified city, 121
frequency of God, 11

giants, 64, 108
gift, 70, 118
glory, 39, 50, 55, 82, 109
goal, 47, 48, 81, 84, 111
God, 11, 13, 14, 15, 16, 17, 18, 19, 20, 21, 22, 23, 24, 25, 26, 28, 30, 32, 33, 35, 38, 39, 41, 42, 43, 45, 46, 47, 48, 49, 50, 51, 52, 53, 54, 55, 57, 59, 62, 63, 64, 67, 68, 72, 73, 74, 75, 77, 78, 79, 80, 81, 82, 83, 84, 85, 87, 88, 89, 90, 91, 92, 93, 94, 95, 106, 107, 108, 109, 110, 111, 112, 113, 114, 116, 119, 120, 121, 122
God's eternal Spirit, 43
God's faith, 43
God's help, 37, 39
God's ideas, 13
God's mercies, 102
God's Spirit, 41, 43, 59
God's thoughts, 13
God's voice, 22, 43
God's word, 41, 47, 49, 50, 51
God's words, 26, 46, 47, 48, 49, 50
God-plans, 120, 121
God's favour, 92
God's instructions, 18
God's plans, 122
God's promises, 32, 33
God's voice, 14, 16, 18, 19, 20, 22, 46, 53, 68
God's ways, 92
God's word, 52, 89, 90, 91, 94
God's words, 68, 88, 90
good spiritual sense, 100
good understanding, 89, 94, 95, 99
grace, 25, 33, 84
gratitude, 102

hardened, 93
healing, 58, 59
hear, 14, 15, 17, 22
heart, 18, 19, 20, 67, 72, 73, 74, 111, 112
hearts, 92, 94
heaven's floodgates, 54, 55
Heaven's floodgates, 54, 59
help, 12, 63, 64, 65, 68, 69, 70, 104
Helper, 66, 68, 70

hidden enemies, 39
His mercies, 102
His Spirit, 38, 67
His voice, 14, 15, 17
His ways, 46, 80, 98, 99, 100
His words, 52, 98, 99
holiness, 81, 82
Holy Spirit, 16, 37, 38, 39, 42, 61, 62, 66, 67, 68, 69, 70, 71, 72, 73, 77, 107, 108, 121, 122
Holy Spirit's revelation, 121
home, 69
hope, 19, 35, 65, 120
Human beings, 117
humble, 74, 84, 93, 94
humility, 70, 81, 109
Humility. *See* humility

idea, 13, 21, 52, 112, 113
ideas, 15, 16, 61, 109, 112, 113, 114, 119
idle, 108, 114
idols, 84
imagination, 59
immortality, 98
In His presence, 67
insecurity, 104
insight, 32, 33, 34
Institutions, 117
instructions, 18, 19, 34, 61, 68, 71, 98, 109
interceding, 89, 102
intimacy with God, 77, 82

intimate fellowship, 88

Jacob, 86
Jehoshaphat, 37, 39
Jericho, 121
Jesus, 12, 13, 17, 29, 30, 50, 72, 82, 102, 114
Jesus Christ, 13, 29, 30, 50, 72, 102, 114
Jonah, 79, 84
Joshua, 103, 121
journey, 32, 64, 66
judgemental, 104

knowledge, 89, 90, 91, 93, 95, 116, 117

labour, 25, 26, 51, 52
leadership, 10, 68
life, 28, 29, 38, 46, 49, 52, 56, 60, 65, 66, 71, 76, 82, 93, 94, 98, 108, 109, 110
limitless possibilities, 23, 27
love, 65, 81, 86, 102, 104
Luke, 60, 85, 87

manifestations, 14, 15
marketplace, 119
marriage, 87
Mary, 13
meditation, 33, 45, 46
meditations, 32, 68, 123
mental faculties, 113, 122
mercies and compassion, 102

merciful, 103
mercy, 10, 84, 103, 104
metamorphose
    transformation, 50
metamorphosis, 90, 91
    transformation, 57
midnight vigils, 11
mind, 14, 15, 16, 17, 20, 42, 46, 61, 89, 91, 93, 94, 114, 122
minds, 15, 92
ministry, 34, 110
miracles, 11, 26, 65, 66, 85
Moses, 10, 11, 47, 52, 99, 121
my life, 96, 99
mysteries, 72, 73, 115

Nations, 59, 117
natural human intellect, 121
natural mind, 120
natural strength, 65
Nineveh, 79

obedience, 74
occupied, 115
offering, 91, 92
oil, 15, 61, 62
opinions, 94
opportunities, 24, 55
opportunity, 92
overflow, 15

parable, 104
parable of the barren tree, 104

patience, 103
patient, 102
patient and tolerant, 102
Paul, 85
Pentecost, 100
personal holiness, 65, 66
personal success, 43
perspectives, 95
Peter, 50, 52, 91, 100
Petitions, 33
Pharaoh, 10
Philippian, 100
plan, 25, 111, 112, 113, 114
planning, 113, 114, 122, 123
Planning, 114
plans, 111, 112, 113, 119
plans and planning, 119
possibilities, 18, 63, 104, 105
potentials, 104
poverty, 60
power, 34, 35, 42, 43, 46, 50, 55, 57, 67, 71, 72, 82, 108, 121
power to *create wealth*, 108
powerful, 17, 28, 29, 33, 37, 48, 68, 73, 113, 119, 121, 122
powerful keys, 28, 33
powers of darkness, 49, 56
practical realities, 119
pragmatic assessment, 119
Praise, 33, 50
pray, 24, 28, 32, 33, 34, 65, 66, 71, 72, 80, 110, 115

pray and fast, 115
pray in the Spirit, 71
prayer, 33, 34, 35, 37, 52, 68, 71, 72, 73, 121
prayer and prophetic warrior, 121
prayers, 17, 22, 33, 35, 36, 68, 71, 72, 73, 107, 123
praying, 11, 17, 28, 29, 30, 31, 32, 33, 34, 35, 36, 53, 71, 72, 73, 79, 83, 106, 107, 108, 109, 113, 116, 119, 121
Praying, 26, 28, 30, 113, 115
PRAYING, 32
praying and fasting, 17, 28, 31, 32, 33, 34, 71, 106, 107, 113
Praying and fasting, 115
praying in the Spirit, 71, 72
praying in tongues, 72
praying saint's advantage, 119
predestined, 97
price, 117, 118
price-tag, 117
pride, 89, 90, 91, 93, 94
priorities, 87
problems, 116, 117
product, 115
productive, 57, 107, 115
productively, 115
productivity, 106, 107, 113, 115, 116, 118, 119, 122, 123

profit, 51, 109, 110, 112, 114, 117, 118
profitability, 107, 115, 118, 122, 123
profitable, 112, 119
profitably, 115
profiting, 110, 113, 119
profits, 110
Promised Land, 63, 103, 104
promises, 32, 100
prophecies, 61, 73, 96, 97, 98, 99, 100, 107
prophecy, 97
Prophecy, 98
prophetic, 11, 32, 33, 65
Prophetic, 31
prophetic declarations, 99
prophetic utterances, 11
prophetic, and spiritual, 121
prophetic/spiritual plans, 119
prosperity, 56, 59, 60, 74, 75, 77, 111
Prosperity, 60
proud, 93
prowess, 64
Psalm, 14, 15, 17, 32
purity, 81, 82, 84

quality, 84, 118
questions, 116
quiet, 17
quietness, 42

rain, 41, 43, 44, 107

Rain, 41
Red Sea, 10, 103
relationships, 69, 80
relevance, 59
religious, 15
renewal, 42
repentance, 33, 79, 80, 84
results, 13, 25, 35, 55, 66, 107
revelations, 46, 85, 97, 109
righteousness, 98

Sacrificial giving, 26
salvation, 48, 107
Samuel, 20, 21
saved, 100
schooling, 69
Scriptural, 33
scriptures, 17, 33
secret, 14, 22, 67
secrets, 16
seek God, 32, 37, 39, 87, 109, 121
sermon, 100
services, 111, 117
settle down, 114, 115
sin, 30, 83
skills, 64, 108, 116, 117
Small businesses, 117
soar on wings, 123
soldiers, 121
solitude, 17, 20, 42, 53, 121, 123
solutions, 10, 14, 26, 117, 118, 122

sound, 21, 22, 41, 43, 44, 112
speaking in tongues, 108
speed, 118, 123
spirit, 14, 26, 29, 31, 33, 44, 46, 61, 68, 72, 109, 119
Spirit of the LORD, 37, 39, 67
Spirit-led, 119
spiritual, 7, 11, 17, 19, 24, 25, 26, 28, 29, 30, 31, 32, 33, 35, 36, 39, 42, 61, 65, 80, 82, 83, 84, 90, 94, 100, 107, 110, 113, 119, 121
Spiritual, 30
spiritual and prophetic insight, 32, 33
spiritual blindness, 94
spiritual disciplines, 26, 121
spiritual insight, 32
spiritual poison, 30, 90
spiritual progress, 43
spiritual warfare, 11
spiritually, 89, 93
stagnant, 43, 93
stagnation, 31, 93, 94
strategies, 26, 120, 121
strength, 57, 63, 64, 65, 66, 67, 68
stubborn, 30, 31, 93
submission, 89
success, 16, 25, 75, 77, 109
sufficient cash, 115
supernatural, 11, 13
supernatural interventions. *See* uncommon solutions

supernatural manifestations, 28, 33, *See* uncommon solutions
miracles, 82
supernatural provisions, 23
supplication, 33
Supplications, 33
surrender, 64, 67, 68
Surrender, 45, 62, 67, 68
survive the sword, 23, 24, 27

talent, 70
talents, 70, 116, 117
the eagle, 123
the earth, 49, 66, 120, 123
the enemy, 39, 41
the fear of God, 74, 75, 76, 77, 78
the flesh, 25, 26, 45, 46, 68
the heavens, 120
the help of God, 63, 70
the human mind, 121
the presence of the Lord, 42
the Spirit, 16, 37, 39, 71, 98, 110
The Spirit of God, 113
the storms of life, 23, 27
the voice of God, 76
the ways of the LORD, 80
the wise, 99
the word, 52, 53, 74
the *work of your hands*, 109, 111, 113
the world, 45, 47, 49, 66, 86, 87
things of the world, 46
this world, 20, 23, 46, 50, 51, 68, 82, 85, 87
thoughts, 93, 94, 120
Timothy, 48, 83, 85, 110
Titus, 85
tolerance, 104
transformation, 57
trust, 39, 64, 65, 70

uncertainties, 69
uncommon results, 13
uncommon solution, 11, 12, 13
uncommon solutions, 5, 11, 13, 14, 17, 18, 22, 23, 27, 38, 39, 43, 58, 61, 63, 66, 71, 76, 79, 80, 81, 88, 94, 95, 99, 101, 105, 107, 121
Uncommon solutions, 11, 28, 33
understanding, 14, 33, 34, 94

values, 87
vision, 34, 89, 90, 112, 120
vision of God, 104
visions, 41
voice of God, 19, 20

warriors, 64
waves of favours, 37
way, 14, 17, 25, 29, 31, 38, 45, 57, 60, 62, 68, 76, 92, 93,

94, 97, 98, 100, 106, 112, 120
ways, 77, 79, 80, 97, 98, 99, 100, 120
weaknesses, 63, 64, 72, 103
wealth, 40, 49, 60, 75, 77, 78, 108, 110, 115
weapons, 28, 29
wisdom, 14, 50, 65, 66, 77, 78, 100, 103, 108, 109, 115
wise plan, 119
word of Christ, 93
words of God, 43, 48, 49
work, 18, 25, 42, 47, 51, 52, 60, 64, 83, 109, 111, 113, 114, 115
worldliness, 85, 87, 88
Worldliness, 20, 85, 86, 87
worries, 41
worship, 22, 52, 67, 68, 72, 88
worshippers, 91

your efforts, 13

your enemies, 38, 59
Your health, 40
your heart, 15, 17, 41, 46, 52, 68, 73, 76, 81, 87, 93, 113, 120
your life, 11, 13, 14, 15, 17, 25, 30, 31, 38, 39, 43, 44, 45, 47, 54, 55, 59, 60, 62, 65, 80, 81, 87, 107, 109, 111, 120
your light, 66
your mind, 13, 15, 16, 86, 87
your mindset, 16, 46
your mouth, 43
your obedience, 13
your own plans, 122
Your plans, 111
your products, 117, 118
your thoughts, 43
your tongue, 43, 73
your words, 61

Also by Pastor WD Favour

Rivers in the Desert

How can your desert be transformed into the Garden of Eden? How can you tap into God's limitless and abundant riches? How would you rise from the dung-heap of failures and frustrations? This book is about the answers to these questions.

Author, Evangelist, and Pastor, Wildfire D. Favour, in this inspirational work, kindles a fiery desire to live above unfruitfulness and failure.

This book shares principles and understanding that would rescue anyone from the pit of mediocrity.

Can God Be Lonely?

Ever since 1994 when WD Favour began to share his encounter with the Holy Spirit on a rainy night in the University of Nigeria, Nsukka, thousands of people have experienced tremendous personal revival in their walk with God.

This booklet contains that life-transforming revelation.

"I am more convinced today than ever before that l communion with God is the one single key that unlocks ighs and supernatural favours." ~ Pastor WD Favour

Healed!

After 17 years of pain, agony, uncertainties, fear, and depression due to debilitating illnesses, WD Favour experienced the miracle of divine healing.

This booklet not only tells that story, it also challenges you to trust God for your healing and that of your loved ones.

The message of this booklet is simple – you too can be HEALED!

Pastor WD Favour is an international preacher with a terrific passion for Jesus Christ. His writings and messages reach over 30,000 people monthly in 72 countries.

www.ingramcontent.com/pod-product-compliance
Lightning Source LLC
Chambersburg PA
CBHW031400040426
42444CB00005B/367